Lucy Lombos

I0157487

FEVERISH

Illustrated by Nisansala Alwis

This is a children's book, published by Lombosco Publications-Canada.

Date Published: December 25, 2023

Illustrated by Nisansala Alwis from Sri Lanka.

Dedication

This book that teaches kids to care for the environment is dedicated to all grade school children and educators in the whole world.

Words to Learn

1. **pygmy-** something that is very small or tiny.

2. **coral reef-** is a great home for animals and plants. It's a ridge (hill or a mountain range) of rock in the sea formed by the growth and deposit of coral; a coral is a horny and stony substance under the sea.

3. **Anacropora puertogalerae-** is a scientific name. It points out to the corals of the world and to the species of briar coral that can be found in the central Indo-Pacific, Japan, the East China Sea, eastern Australia, the oceanic west Pacific Ocean, the Philippines and the Maldives. It is also found in the Andaman Islands, Rodrigues, Fiji and Vanuatu. It occurs in shallow reefs, from depths of 5–20 m. It is very fragile and is particularly susceptible to coral bleaching, disease and habitat loss.

4. **climate change-** a change in global or regional climate patterns, in particular a change from the mid to late 20th century onwards and caused by the rising levels of atmospheric carbon dioxide which is produced using fossil fuels.

5. **global warming-** a slow increase in the overall temperature of the earth's atmosphere attributed to the greenhouse effect caused by rising levels of carbon dioxide and other pollutants.

6. **greenhouse effect-** the trapping of the sun's warmth in a planet's lower atmosphere

7. **fossil fuels-** a natural fuel such as coal or gas, also oil, formed in the geological past from the remains of living organisms.

8. **deforestation-** the action of clearing a wide area of trees; simply, it means cutting of trees.

9. **solar farm-** an area of land in which a large number of solar panels are set up in order to generate electricity.

10. **wind turbine-** a turbine (a machine) having a large vaned wheel rotated by the wind to generate electricity.

11. **geothermal energy-** is heat that is generated within the earth. It is a renewable resource that can be harvested for human use - for cooking, bathing, space heating, electrical power generation, and other uses.

12. **hydropower plant-** is the electricity produced from generators driven by turbines that convert the potential energy of falling or fast-flowing water into mechanical energy.

13. **Reduce, Reuse, Recycle-** known as the 3 R's. It's a campaign to use natural resources wisely. It encourages people to waste less, use less and use things again to protect the environment.

14. **land reclamation-** is done by adding material such as rocks, soil and cement to an area of water; submerging wetlands, covering and overflowing the waters.

15. **carbon emissions-** refer to the carbon dioxide that planes, cars, factories and others produce or sent out. They are harmful to the environment.

Pretty surprising! Like humans, sea creatures also think of their summer vacation.

"Would you like to go to the other coral reef?" Wisey, the pygmy seahorse with a purple color and spots of white, asked his friend.

"Oh boy, that's cool! Let's go!" Smarty, a green pygmy seahorse speckled with gold and stripes of orange, replied.

The two seahorse friends had been staying at Apo Reef in Sablayan, Occidental Mindoro when they considered spending their summer break in Puerto Galera, Oriental Mindoro.

"Time to enjoy Puerto Galera's coral reefs!" Wisey zipped up.

"It's exciting! Being one of the World's Most Beautiful Bays, its coral reefs are famous!" Smarty noted.

"That's why it is also named the Diving Capital of the Philippines."

"Awesome!... I'm ready!"

Smoothing the way for their adventure, they heard the bad news from the giant clam, their newscaster, that a part of their destination's coral reef was destroyed by the boatmen due to the careless dropping of anchors, causing dangers to the sea creatures. Also, human divers' irresponsibility causes the destruction of the marine ecosystem and the creatures' death.

So, Wisey and Smarty postponed their vacation. But days later, they decided to carry out their plan.

"I can't wait to see the renowned Anacropora puertogalerae!" Wisey boasted.

"Me, too! Nice scientific name, eh!" Smarty said.

Another news held them back. They heard from the giant clam there would be a super typhoon.

"Too bad! We need to wait again till the typhoon disappears."

"It's okay. It's for our safety."

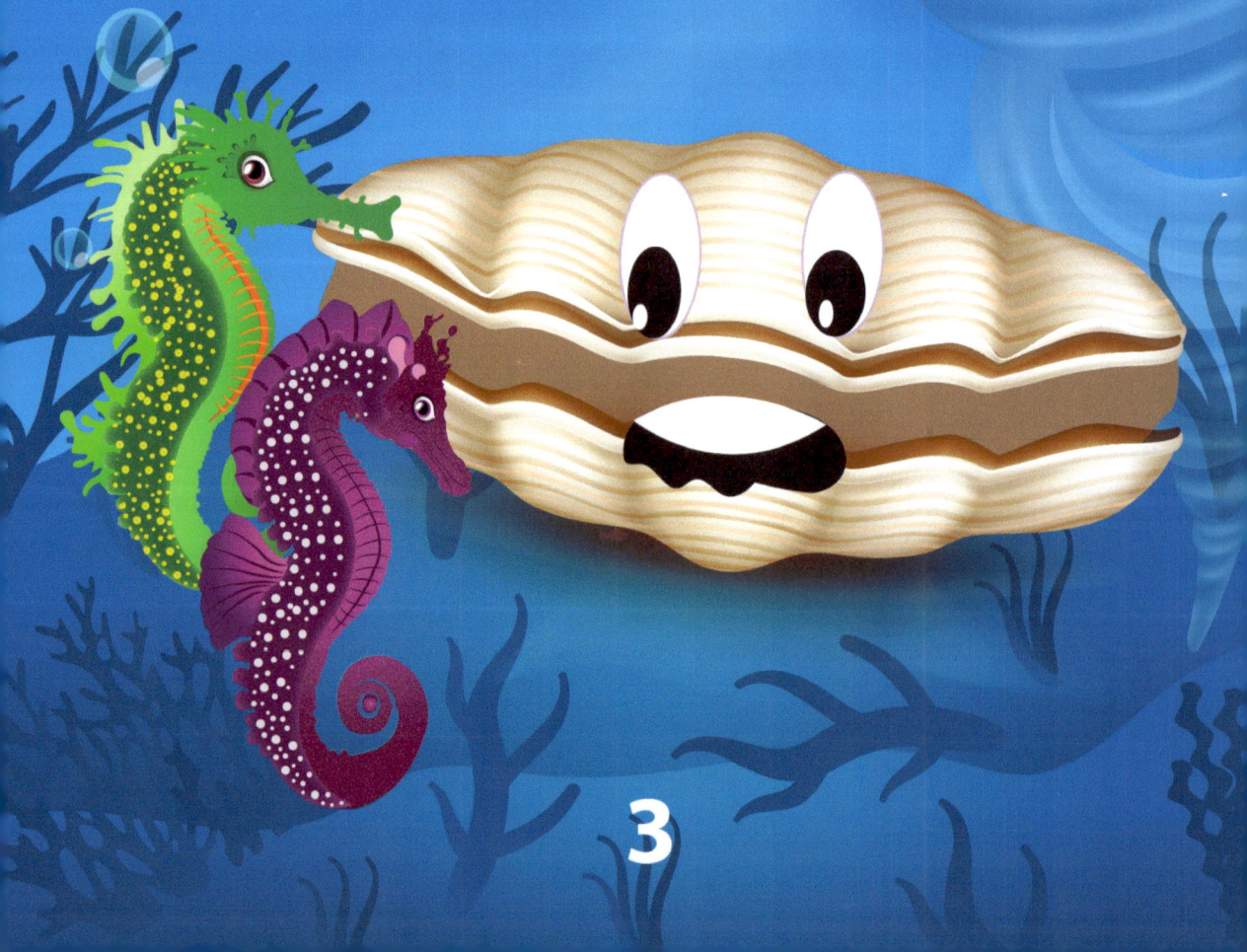

The typhoon surge that hurtled towards the Tagalog provinces caused the big ship, carrying thousands of liters of oil, to sink off Naujan, Oriental Mindoro. The oil spillage spread in Mindoro's neighboring towns.

This disaster stopped the seahorse friends from having their vacation.

"Oh, humans, you brought this massive trouble to our seas again," Wisey quipped while Smarty listened in dismay.

But not so long, nothing could stop them. Although the seahorses could slowly swim, they still decided to propel their bodies through the waters.

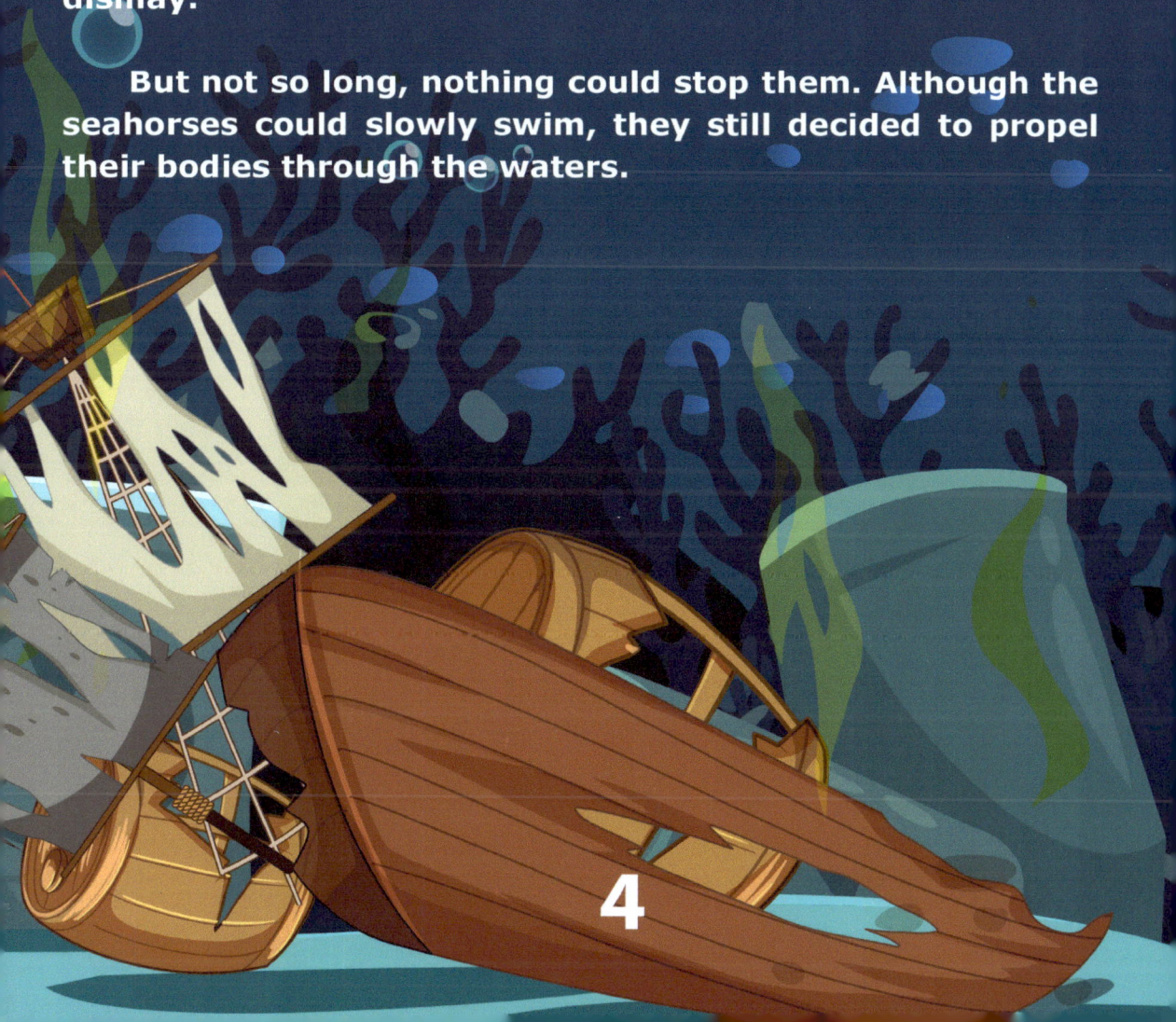

Smarty said, "Ugh! I'm a bit nauseous. Maybe, I have eaten something contaminated with the toxic oil."

"Gosh! Spit it out!"

"Don't worry, I will be fine."

"Take it easy! We are already far off."

Smarty asked, "Any news?"

"It's sad. Our Mother Earth is feverish!" Wisey replied.

"Feverish? Big word! The Earth has a high temperature, right?" Smarty asked.

Climate Change
Global Warming

"Yes, it's all about climate change and this thing called global warming!" Wisey said.

"Yeah, it's climate change, the long-term variations or shifts in temperatures and weather patterns," Smarty explained and asked later, "Aaah, humans don't take care of our home planet! Because of their inventions and activities, everything has become a crisis. What must be done?"

"First, they must stop or reduce the earth's fever!"

"Please share your idea of global warming."

"Global warming is the term used to describe the rising of the earth's temperature," Wisey defined.

"Well said!" Smarty remarked and detailed out, "Based on my readings, it's the process of the planet heating up. So many years ago, it was warmed by 1°C, and scientists predicted the earth's temperature might go up from from 2% to 5%. Do you know the primary cause of global warming?" asked Smarty.

Wisey made clear, "The greenhouse effect is the leading cause of global warming."

Smarty admired Wisey's quick answer and presented, "The greenhouse effect is a way of trapping the sun's warmth in the atmosphere. The trapped gases are like a blanket we cannot see, but they cover and wrap all of us. These trapped gases- carbon dioxide, methane, nitrous oxides, and water vapor- keep Mother Earth hotter and hotter. I'm afraid we will all be roasted here."

"Excellent insights!... Climate change has sped up since the beginning of the industrial age. Humans have been burning huge amounts of fossil fuels, known as oil and gases. The gas is released to our atmosphere, but it acts as a shield, as you've said, a "blanket," preventing our planet from cooling down," Wisey simplified.

They mentioned another global warming cause, and that's deforestation. The trees absorb carbon dioxide from the air and release it back into the air as oxygen. If the trees are cut, the carbon dioxide is not used up anymore, making it stay and gather in the atmosphere. Thus, warming the globe.

"Humans must plant trees!" Smarty popped a critical action to do.

"That's important! Planting trees can make the earth cool and green. We need more of them. They take in lots of carbon dioxide, the air humans exhale, and the gas produced by burning carbon and organic compounds," Wisey discussed.

"Make sense! What else can humans do to save the planet? Hmmm...," Smarty started thinking when Wisey added, "They should not throw garbage on the seas and other water forms."

"You're a genius! Air, land, and water pollution has been everybody's suffering. They are destroying everything and killing everyone. Well, I heard from the mixed shoals of different aquatic species that fish kill, or the sudden deaths of the fish, is also rooted in the improper and imprudent garbage disposal to the seas and oceans."

"Exactly, Smarty!" Wisey exclaimed. "Also, they should not waste energy."

"Energy! ... I agree! Humans must turn off the lights and other electrical appliances when unnecessary."

"Correct! Don't dig the lands and do illegal mining just to get coals to run the industrial factories, agricultural warehouses and other kinds of businesses along with the vehicles, appliances, other products and services consumed by the offices, institutions, including houses," Wisey explained.

"Indeed, the coals are used as fuels to generate electric power," Smarty said. "Never waste energy! Humans must look for alternative renewable energy sources to prevent too much dependence on digging and mining coals."

10

"That's true! They can build solar farms, wind turbines, geothermal energy, hydropower plant, and many more substitutes," Wisey informed.

"Geesh, there are many things to study, discover, and teach others to stop the planet's fever," Smarty said. "By the way, are we there yet?"

"Even if we move like snails, we're more than halfway... Hurry, swim fast! The foreign fishermen are here to get us for their food and medicines," Wisey warned.

11

"Oh my! They love to catch us for their own advantage," Smarty complained.

"Hence, we are now few."

"Endangered, Wisey!"

They tried to flip their fins fast, moving up, down, and forward.

"Whew, we are far from them now!" the twain calmed down.

Wisey and Smarty continued talking.

12

"Oh, I remember the 'Reduce, Reuse and Recycle' campaign!" Smarty shared.

"Brilliant mind! Humans must keep this widespread campaign going," Wisey agreed.

"There's another thing they must do. Climate change is linked to water. Water can fight off the crisis and lessen carbon emissions. Each will feel its necessity when floods, rising sea levels, snow melting, wildfires and droughts occur. Never waste water as well," Smarty expounded.

13

"Let's go and announce all these things to our friends!" Wisey said and reminded, "But we have to enjoy our vacation first!"

"We can do both!" Smarty suggested.

They arrived safely and enjoyed the colorful rainforest of the sea in Puerto Galera.

They met Sharpie, the stealthy, rainbow-colored seahorse who talked about the reclamation or landfill.

"Policymakers must control humans' activities in creating new land from water forms. The waters are compressed and would flow anywhere because they are displaced. The heat is intensified in the water," Sharpie contributed.

"Great topic! Problems arise and ruin our homeland because of reclamation, too!" Wisey affirmed.

"Everyone will die if humans don't take immediate action," Smarty got worried.

While touring and sharing their thoughts with their new friend, they promised to stop Mother Earth's fever.

"Everyone has a role to play and contribute," Sharpie continued, "We, fish, can save the world by helping store carbon dioxide in the waters."

15

"I heard that somewhere! We need experts to discuss this serious matter," Smarty said.

"Sounds great!" Sharpie blurted.

"We can swim up on the water's surface and check what's happening on the food web. Then, let's deepen our knowledge on carbon emissions," Smarty spelled out.

"Perfect! We can figure out how to take carbon dioxide as our captives into the oceans. By understanding science concepts, we can take them away on the surface," Wisey pitched in.

"Let's do this!" Sharpie hastened them. Afterward, she sensed the fishermen's arrival. She swam at the interior of the coral reef, leading and protecting other friends.

Likewise, Wisey and Smarty swam and hid themselves. When those men left, they made a pinky-swear by crisscrossing their curly tails.

Later, they swam farther to spread global warming awareness to their friends.

They believe living things grow and thrive when each one cares for the earth.

They wished for more fun, safe, and healthy summer vacations.

~The End~

*** The Author ***

Hi! **Lucy E. Lombos** is the author of this environmental children's book. Each letter of her first name has meaning.

L- Light. Yes, that's right, the bubbly light of the family! She is a loving daughter and sister, a wife, a mom of three sweethopes, a grandma of her first sweetjoy, a jolly friend and a dedicated teacher. She always asks the Holy Spirit to enlighten her mind, to inspire her and guide her all the time. Praise God! Modesty aside, she graduated with Honors- Valedictorian in Elementary, Silver Medalist with General Excellence Award in High School and Cum Laude in College. She had a religious education and formation at Don Bosco Seminary College, and graduated at the Divine Word College of Calapan, SVD. In De La Salle University, Taft, Manila, she pursued her graduate studies; and completed the academic units at the University of the Philippines where she specialized in Language and Literacy. She further enhanced her English proficiency skills by enrolling in TESOL (Teaching English to Speakers of Other Languages) with Practicum Course in British Columbia, Canada where she obtained a very high grade.

U- Understanding. Lucy has a substantial and deep understanding of her profession. She undertakes teaching the English fundamental skills, and these are – Speaking, Reading, Writing and Listening. In 2000, she founded Lombosco Academy in the Philippines and she remains the Academy Directress, and the Editor-In-Chief of its Newsletter.

C- Children. They are the subject of her craft. She studied courses about Writing for Children and Writing a Life Story in Canada. She also earned a Diploma in Child Psychology in USA. Her love for children doesn't stop, and so she studied Child Protection: Children's Rights in Theory and Practice, an online course in Harvard University during the peak of the Covid-19 pandemic.

Y- Young. Lucy is always young at heart. She would like to learn more, that's why she never stops resting on her laurels. Further, she is a member of SCBWI- Society of Children's Book Writers and Illustrators, ILA- International Literacy Association and CCCF- Canadian Child Care Federation. She also enjoys blogging, contributing articles for different media and doing educational vlogs.

*N.B. *Lucy taught at Puerto Galera Academy after her College Graduation; and became the Principal at Prince of Peace Montessori, Puerto Galera. *She received two, official recognitions for promoting the Tourism in Puerto Galera, Or. Mindoro, Philippines to the International Level through her authored books in March 2018, and in the following year. *On February 26, 2023, she became a Finalist in the 2023 Woman of Worth Worldwide, held in Marriott Hotel, Burnaby, BC, Canada. Exactly after one month, she was featured in the Gallery Walk for the 77th SVD's Founding Anniversary and listed as one of the 5 Distinguished Personalities in 2023.*

In addition, Lucy received two more awards. On November 3, 2023, the World's Most Beautiful Bays-Puerto Galera Chapter recognized her through a Board Resolution led by Hubert d'Aboville. Then, on November 6, 2023, she received a Certificate of Recognition from the Municipality of Puerto Galera, Philippines, led by Mayor Rocky D. Ilagan.

Bibliography

<u>Lucy Lombos' Published Books on Amazon</u>

1. *Ang Tinago Kong Piso/The Peso-Coin I Kept (Bilingual)*

2. *The Class Lady Bug*

3. *The Star of the Sea: A Boat Ride*

4. *Happiness 365 and ¼ Days (a biography)*

5. *'Ter and Ter', the Turtle and the Eagle*

6. *The Joys of Junior*

7. *Swanie's Bag*

8. *Rose of Calapan (a novel)*

9. *Bono (an early chapter book)*

10. *Three Fables, Part 1: Keys to Change the Heart*

11. *Three Fables, Part 2: Sparks to Brighten One's Purpose in Life*

12. *Pinky Oinky*

13. *Gracie and Dots*

14. *Noshi*

15. *After Six o' Clock Nightfall (short stories quadrilogy)*

16. *One Drop, Two Drops and Much More*

17. *Ellie-Phant and Mon-Keysha*

18. *Monsters in Lazareto (folktales)*

19. *Ely's Gift (an early chapter book)*

20. *Cotton and Nibbles*

21. *Beary G*

22. *Love, Fishbeak*

23. *Like the Sand and Like the Living Rock (a coloring book for kids)*

24. *Wednesday*

25. *Solana*

26. *The String of Saga Seeds (a novel)*

27. *Wiz Jordy's Magic Words*

28. *Rock Bottom Stories and Prayers (religious and inspirational)*

29. *Caffeinated Short Stories*

30. *Contributor to Theresa Jacobs' Self-Help Book: Writing 101, How to Write for Yourself & Share with the World.*

31. *Peachy and Pinky ~Purring Together~*

32. *Feverish- the book you're reading now.*

33. *Echo and Light Poetry Anthology*

34. *LEMONstacular Short Stories MiniParade*

*** Her upcoming book ***

35. *Nature Walk: Encounters and Reflections*

*** Acknowledgment ***

I would like to express my deep gratitude to the following people for giving me the big support which I humbly needed in writing this book –

Umberto Lombos, Jr. for publishing this book;

Ely, my mom and the entire family for giving me the moral support in my writing ministry;

Daniel Enriquez for helping me editing the scientific part of the book;

To the blurb writers,

Marine Walick,

Daniel Enriquez

and

Gem Balajadia-Lombos

I am truly amazed and grateful to you all.

- Lucy Lombos

www.ingramcontent.com/pod-product-compliance
Lightning Source LLC
Chambersburg PA
CBHW042110040426
42448CB00002B/212